CW01457763

There is ... only a single categorical imperative and it is this: Act only on that maxim through which you can at the same time will that it should become a universal law.

Two things fill the mind with ever new and increasing admiration and awe, the oftener and the more steadily we reflect on them: the starry heavens above and the moral law within.

The light dove, in free flight cutting through the air the resistance of which it feels, could get the idea that it could do even better in airless space. Likewise, Plato abandoned the world of the senses because it posed so many hindrances for the understanding, and dared to go beyond it on the wings of the ideas, in the empty space of pure understanding.

Of all the arts poetry
(which owes its origin
almost entirely to
genius and will least
be guided by precept
or example) maintains
the first rank.

Have patience awhile; slanders are not long-lived. Truth is the child of time; erelong she shall appear to vindicate thee.

Do what is right,
though the world
may perish.

It is so easy to be immature. If I have a book to serve as my understanding,
a pastor to serve as my conscience, a physician to determine my diet for me, and so on, I need not exert myself at all.
I need not think, if only I can pay: others will readily undertake the irksome work for me.

The evil effect of
science upon men is
principally this, that
by far the greatest
number of those who wish
to display a knowledge
of it accomplish no
improvement at all of the
understanding, but only
a perversity of it, not to
mention that it serves
most of them as a tool of
vanity.

As everybody likes to
be honored, so people
imagine that God also
wants to be honored.
They forget that the
fulfillment of duty
towards men is the only
honor adequate to him.

The greatest problem for the human race, to the solution of which Nature drives man, is the achievement of a universal civic society which administers law among men.

Criticism alone can sever the root of materialism, fatalism, atheism, free-thinking, fanaticism, and superstition, which can be injurious universally; as well as of idealism and skepticism, which are dangerous chiefly to the Schools, and hardly allow of being handed on to the public.

Morality is not
properly the
doctrine of how we
may make ourselves
happy, but how we
may make ourselves
worthy of happiness.

Man's greatest concern
is to know how he shall
properly fill his place
in the universe and
correctly understand
what he must be in
order to be a man.

The ideal of the supreme being is nothing but a regulative principle of reason which directs us to look upon all connection in the world as if it originated from an all-sufficient necessary cause.

Good and strong will.
Mechanism must
precede science
(learning). Also in
morals and religion?
Too much discipline
makes one narrow and
kills proficiency.
Politeness belongs,
not to discipline,
but to polish, and
thus comes last.

The guidelines for
achieving wisdom
consist of three
leading maxims:

1) Think for yourself;

2) (in communication
with other people) Put
yourself in the place
of the other person;

3) Always think by
remaining faithful
to your own self.

When a thoughtful
human being has
overcome incentives
to vice and is aware of
having done his bitter
duty, he finds himself
in a state that could
be called happiness, a
state of contentment
and peace of mind in
which virtue is its
own reward.

Aristotle can be regarded as the father of logic. But his logic is too scholastic, full of subtleties, and fundamentally has not been of much value to the human understanding. It is a dialectic and an organon for the art of disputation.

All human
knowledge begins
with intuitions,
proceeds from
thence to concepts,
and ends with ideas.

To a high degree we
are, through art and
science, cultured.
We are civilized —
perhaps too much for
our own good — in all
sorts of social grace
and decorum. But to
consider ourselves
as having reached
morality — for that,
much is lacking.

A mind of slow
apprehension
is therefore not
necessarily a weak
mind. The one
who is alert with
abstractions is not
always profound,
he is more often
very superficial.

As to moral feeling, this supposed special sense, the appeal to it is indeed superficial when those who cannot think believe that feeling will help them out, even in what concerns general laws: and besides, feelings which naturally differ infinitely in degree cannot furnish a uniform standard of good and evil, nor has any one a right to form judgments for others by his own feelings....

Metaphysics has as the proper object of its enquiries three ideas only: God, freedom, and immortality.

What alone has value
is the use to which
life is put and the
end to which it is
directed. The value of
life has to be created
by man, it cannot be
obtained through
luck but only through
wisdom. He who is
anxiously concerned
over losing his life
will never enjoy life.

But only he who, himself enlightened, is not afraid of shadows.

(An Answer to the Question: What Is Enlightenment?)

It is therefore correct to say that the senses do not err — not because they always judge rightly, but because they do not judge at all.

The child must be brought up free (that he allow others to be free). He must learn to endure the restraint to which freedom subjects itself for its own preservation (experience no subordination to his command). Thus he must be disciplined. This precedes instruction. Training must continue without interruption. He must learn to do without things and to be cheerful about it. He must not be obliged to dissimulate, he must acquire immediate horror of lies, must learn so to respect the rights of men that they become an insurmountable wall for him. His instruction must be more negative. He must not learn religion before he knows morality. He must be refined, but not spoiled (pampered). He must learn to speak frankly, and must assume no false shame. Before adolescence he must not learn fine manners; thoroughness is the chief thing. Thus he is crude longer, but earlier useful and capable.

Man's duty is to improve himself; to cultivate his mind; and, when he finds himself going astray, to bring the moral law to bear upon himself.

Only the descent
into the hell of
self-knowledge
can pave the way
to godliness.

The more one presupposes
that his own power will
suffice him to realize
what he desires the more
practical is that desire.
When I treat a man
contemptuously, I can
inspire him with no
practical desire to
appreciate my grounds of
truth. When I treat any
one as worthless, I can
inspire him with no
desire to do right.

In the kingdom of ends
everything has either
a price or a dignity.
What has a price can be
replaced by something
else as its equivalent;
what on the other hand
is raised above all
price and therefore
admits of no
equivalent
has a dignity.

Beneficence is a duty. He who often practices this, and sees his beneficent purpose succeed, comes at last really to love him whom he has benefited. When, therefore, it is said, "Thou shalt love thy neighbor as thyself," this does not mean, "Thou shalt first of all love, and by means of love (in the next place) do him good"; but: "Do good to thy neighbour, and this beneficence will produce in thee the love of men (as a settled habit of inclination to beneficence)."

Since the narrower or wider community of the peoples of the earth has developed so far that a violation of rights in one place is felt throughout the world, the idea of a cosmopolitan right is not fantastical, high-flown or exaggerated notion. It is a complement to the unwritten code of the civil and international law, necessary for the public rights of mankind in general and thus for the realization of perpetual peace.

The master is
himself an animal,
and needs a master.

Freedom is independence
of the compulsory will of
another, and in so far as
it tends to exist with
the freedom of all
according to a universal
law, it is the one sole
original inborn right
belonging to every man
in virtue of his
humanity.

In all judgements by
which we describe
anything as beautiful,
we allow no one to be
of another opinion.

Nature does nothing in vain, and in the use of means to her goals she is not prodigal. Her giving to man reason and the freedom of the will which depends upon it is clear indication of her purpose. Man accordingly was not to be guided by instinct, not nurtured and instructed with ready-made knowledge; rather, he should bring forth everything out of his own resources.

The science of mathematics presents the most brilliant example of how pure reason may successfully enlarge its domain without the aid of experience.

All false art, all
vain wisdom, lasts
its time but finally
destroys itself, and
its highest culture
is also the epoch of
its decay.

I am an investigator by inclination. I feel a great thirst for knowledge and an impatient eagerness to advance, also satisfaction at each progressive step. There was a time when I thought that all this could constitute the honor of humanity, and I despised the mob, which knows nothing about it. Rousseau set me straight. This dazzling excellence vanishes; I learn to honor men, and would consider myself much less useful than common laborers if I did not believe that this consideration could give all the others a value, to establish the rights of humanity.

Human reason has
this peculiar fate
that in one species
of its knowledge
it is burdened by
questions which, as
prescribed by the
very nature of reason
itself, it is not able
to ignore, but which,
as transcending all
its powers, it is also
not able to answer.

All thought must, directly or indirectly, by way of certain characters, relate ultimately to intuitions, and therefore, with us, to sensibility, because in no other way can an object be given to us.

The guardians who have kindly undertaken the supervision will see to it that by far the largest part of mankind, including the entire "beautiful sex," should consider the step into maturity, not only as difficult but as very dangerous.

After having made their domestic animals dumb and having carefully prevented these quiet creatures from daring to take any step beyond the lead-strings to which they have fastened them, these guardians then show them the danger which threatens them, should they attempt to walk alone.

God has put a secret
art into the forces of
nature so as to enable
it to fashion itself
out of chaos into a
perfect world system.

A lie is the abandonment and, as it were, the annihilation of the dignity by man. A man who himself does not believe what he tells another ... has even less worth than if he were a mere thing. ... makes himself a mere deceptive appearance of man, not man himself.

Psychologists
have hitherto
failed to realize
that imagination
is a necessary
ingredient of
perception
itself.

There must be a seed of every good thing in the character of men, otherwise no one can bring it out. Lacking that, analogous motives, honor, etc., are substituted. Parents are in the habit of looking out for the inclinations, for the talents and dexterity, perhaps for the disposition of their children, and not at all for their heart or character.

Enlightenment is man's leaving his self-caused immaturity. Immaturity is the incapacity to use one's intelligence without the guidance of another. Such immaturity is self-caused if it is not caused by lack of intelligence, but by lack of determination and courage to use one's intelligence without being guided by another. Sapere Aude! Have the courage to use your own intelligence! is therefore the motto of the enlightenment.

Reason in a creature is a faculty of widening the rules and purposes of the use of all its powers far beyond natural instinct; it acknowledges no limits to its projects. Reason itself does not work instinctively, but requires trial, practice, and instruction in order gradually to progress from one level of insight to another.

Act in such a way that you treat humanity, whether in your own person or in the person of any other, never merely as a means to an end, but always at the same time as an end.

Man has his own inclinations and a natural will which, in his actions, by means of his free choice, he follows and directs. There can be nothing more dreadful than that the actions of one man should be subject to the will of another; hence no abhorrence can be more natural than that which a man has for slavery. And it is for this reason that a child cries and becomes embittered when he must do what others wish, when no one has taken the trouble to make it agreeable to him. He wants to be a man soon, so that he can do as he himself likes.

Among all nations,
through the darkest
polytheism glimmer
some faint sparks of
monotheism.

In every study of
nature there can be
only so much genuine
science as there is a
priori knowledge, by
the same token, natural
philosophy will
contain genuine
science only to the
extent in which
mathematics can be
applied to it.

Philosophical knowledge is the knowledge gained by reason from concepts; mathematical knowledge is the knowledge gained by reason from the construction of concepts.

Through laziness and cowardice a large part of mankind, even after nature has freed them from alien guidance, gladly remain immature. It is because of laziness and cowardice that it is so easy for others to usurp the role of guardians. It is so comfortable to be a minor!

Parents usually educate their children merely in such a manner that however bad the world may be, they may adapt themselves to its present conditions. But they ought to give them an education so much better than this, that a better condition of things may thereby be brought about by the future.

If you punish a child for being naughty, and reward him for being good, he will do right merely for the sake of the reward; and when he goes out into the world and finds that goodness is not always rewarded, nor wickedness always punished, he will grow into a man who only thinks about how he may get on in the world, and does right or wrong according as he finds advantage to himself.

Our knowledge springs from two fundamental sources of the mind; the first is the capacity of receiving representations (receptivity for impressions), the second is the power of knowing an object through these representations (spontaneity [in the production] of concepts).

Is it reasonable to
assume a purposiveness
in all the parts of
nature and to deny it
to the whole?

If education is to
develop human nature
so that it may attain
the object of its
being, it must
involve the
exercise of
judgment.

If it were possible for us to have so deep an insight into a man's character as shown both in inner and in outer actions, that every, even the least, incentive to these actions and all external occasions which affect them were so known to us that his future conduct could be predicted with as great a certainty as the occurrence of a solar or lunar eclipse, we could nevertheless still assert that the man is free.

A public can only arrive at enlightenment slowly. Through revolution, the abandonment of personal despotism may be engendered and the end of profit-seeking and domineering oppression may occur, but never a true reform of the state of mind. Instead, new prejudices, just like the old ones, will serve as the guiding reins of the great, unthinking mass.

All that is required for this enlightenment is freedom; and particularly the least harmful of all that may be called freedom, namely, the freedom for man to make public use of his reason in all matters. But I hear people clamor on all sides: Don't argue! The officer says: Don't argue, drill! The tax collector: Don't argue, pay! The pastor: Don't argue, believe!

The friction among
men, the inevitable
antagonism, which is
a mark of even the
largest societies and
political bodies, is
used by Nature as a
means to establish a
condition of quiet
and security.

Things which we see
are not by themselves
what we see...
It remains completely
unknown to us what the
objects may be by
themselves and apart
from the receptivity of
our senses. We know
nothing but our manner
of perceiving them.

Often war is waged only in order to show valor; thus an inner dignity is ascribed to war itself, and even some philosophers have praised it as an ennoblement of humanity, forgetting the pronouncement of the Greek who said, 'War is an evil in as much as it produces more wicked men than it takes away.'

All the interests of my reason, speculative as well as practical, combine in the three following questions:

1. What can I know?

2. What ought I to do?

3. What may I hope?

I have no knowledge
of myself as I am,
but merely as I
appear to myself.

A metaphysics of morals is therefore indispensably necessary, not merely because of a motive to speculation — for investigating the source of the practical basic principles that lie a priori in our reason — but also because morals themselves remain subject to all sorts of corruption as long as we are without that clue and supreme norm by which to appraise them correctly...

Character means that the person derives his rules of conduct from himself and from the dignity of humanity. Character is the common ruling principle in man in the use of his talents and attributes. Thus it is the nature of his will, and is good or bad. A man who acts without settled principles, with no uniformity, has no character. A man may have a good heart and yet no character, because he is dependent upon impulses and does not act according to maxims. Firmness and unity of principle are essential to character.

No-one can compel me to be happy in accordance with his conception of the welfare of others, for each may seek his happiness in whatever way he sees fit, so long as he does not infringe upon the freedom of others to pursue a similar end which can be reconciled with the freedom of everyone else within a workable general law ? i.e. he must accord to others the same right as he enjoys himself.

It is extremely
absurd to expect to
be enlightened by
reason, and yet to
prescribe to her
beforehand on which
side she must
incline.

To require that a so-called layman should not use his own reason in religious matters, particularly since religion is to be appreciated as moral, but instead follow the appointed clergyman and thus someone else's reason, is an unjust demand because as to morals every man must account for all his doings. The clergyman will not and even cannot assume such a responsibility.

There will always be some people who think for themselves, even among the self-appointed guardians of the great mass who, after having thrown off the yoke of immaturity themselves, will spread about them the spirit of a reasonable estimate of their own value and of the need for every man to think for himself.

Young man! Deny yourself satisfaction (of amusement, of debauchery, of love, etc.), not with the Stoical intention of complete abstinence, but with the refined Epicurean intention of having in view an ever-growing pleasure. This stinginess with the cash of your vital urge makes you definitely richer through the postponement of pleasure, even if you should, for the most part, renounce the indulgence of it until the end of your life. The awareness of having pleasure under your control is, like everything idealistic, more fruitful and more abundant than everything that satisfies the sense through indulgence because it is thereby simultaneously consumed and consequently lost from the aggregate of totality.

We see that scattered through space out to infinite distances, there exist similar systems of stars, and that creation, in the whole extent of its infinite grandeur, is everywhere organized into systems whose members are in relation with one another.... A vast field lies open to discoveries, and observations alone will give the key.

If a man is often the
subject of conversation
he soon becomes the
subject of criticism.

The sum total of all
possible knowledge of
God is not possible
for a human being,
not even through a
true revelation.
But it is one of the
worthiest inquiries
to see how far our
reason can go in the
knowledge of God.

All cognition of
things from mere
pure understanding
and reason is
nothing but mere
illusion and only
in experience is
there truth.

It is absurd ... to
hope that maybe
another Newton may
some day arise, to
make intelligible to
us even the genesis of
but a blade of grass.

I freely admit that the remembrance of David Hume was the very thing that many years ago first interrupted my dogmatic slumber and gave a completely different direction to my researches in the field of speculative philosophy.

[Religion should be]
successively freed
from all statutes
based on history,
and one purely moral
religion rule over
all, in order that God
might be all in all.
The veil must fall.

The inscrutable wisdom through which we exist is not less worthy of veneration in respect to what it denies us than in respect to what it has granted.

Perhaps a revolution
can overthrow
autocratic despotism
and profiteering
or power-grabbing
oppression, but it can
never truly reform a
manner of thinking;
instead, new prejudices,
just like the old ones
they replace, will serve
as a leash for the great
unthinking mass.

I had therefore to
remove knowledge,
in order to make
room for belief.

The only objects of
practical reason are
therefore those of
good and evil. For by
the former is meant
an object necessarily
desired according to a
principle of reason;
by the latter one
necessarily shunned,
also according to a
principle of reason.

Deaths, births, and marriages, considering how much they are separately dependent on the freedom of the human will, should seem to be subject to no law according to which any calculation could be made beforehand of their amount; and yet the yearly registers of these events in great countries prove that they go on with as much conformity to the laws of nature as the oscillations of the weather.

The history of mankind can be seen, in the large, as the realization of Nature's secret plan to bring forth a perfectly constituted state as the only condition in which the capacities of mankind can be fully developed, and also bring forth that external relation among states which is perfectly adequate to this end.

Apart from moral conduct, all that man thinks himself able to do in order to become acceptable to God is mere superstition and religious folly.

Philosophy stands in
need of a science
which shall
determine the
possibility,
principles, and
extent of human
knowledge à priori.

If, like Hume, I had all manner of adornment in my power, I would still have reservations about using them. It is true that some readers will be scared off by dryness. But isn't it necessary to scare off some if in their case the matter would end up in bad hands?

Each according to
his own way of
seeing things,
seek one goal, that
is gratification.

Everything good
that is not based
on a morally good
disposition,
however, is
nothing but
pretense and
glittering misery.

Nothing in the world—
indeed nothing even
beyond the world—can
possibly be conceived
which could be called
good without
qualification
except a good will.

The public use of a man's reason must be free at all times, and this alone can bring enlightenment among men...

Whereas the beautiful is limited, the sublime is limitless, so that the mind in the presence of the sublime, attempting to imagine what it cannot, has pain in the failure but pleasure in contemplating the immensity of the attempt.

....Happiness is not an ideal of reason but of imagination, resting solely on empirical grounds, and it is vain to expect that these should define an action by which one could attain the totality of a series of consequences which is really endless.

The question here is not, "How conscience ought to be guided?" For Conscience is its own General and Leader; it is therefore enough that each man have one. What we want to know is, how conscience can be her own Ariadne.

There is
something
splendid about
innocence; but
what is bad about
it, in turn, is
that it cannot
protect itself
very well and is
easily seduced.

The problem of establishing a perfect civic constitution is dependent upon the problem of a lawful external relation among states and cannot be solved without a solution of the latter problem.

Human freedom is
realised in the adoption
of humanity as an end in
itself, for the one thing
that no-one can be
compelled to do by
another is to adopt
a particular end.

Freedom in the
practical sense is
the independence of
the power of choice
from necessitation
by impulses of
sensibility.

Thoughts without content are empty, intuitions without concepts are blind. The understanding can intuit nothing, the senses can think nothing. Only through their unison can knowledge arise.

One who makes
himself a worm
cannot complain
afterwards if
people step on him.

For how is it possible, says that acute man, that when a concept is given me, I can go beyond it and connect with it another which is not contained in it, in such a manner as if that latter necessarily belonged to the former?

There is an imperative which commands a certain conduct immediately, without having as its condition any other purpose to be attained by it. This imperative is Categorical...This imperative may be called that of Morality.

The enjoyment of power inevitably corrupts the judgment of reason, and perverts its liberty.

Reason must approach nature in order to be taught by it. It must not, however, do so in the character of a pupil who listens to everything that the teacher chooses to say, but of an appointed judge who compels the witness to answer questions which he has himself formulated.

Printed in Great Britain
by Amazon

19298623R10064